What a fabulous book! This book gives parents, family members, teachers, and counselors the opportunity to learn how to create a Friends Group, with an easy, straight-forward process, specific recommendations and examples. The depth of Linda Thalheimer's insight, sensitivity, supportive and corrective means of encouraging group members to develop the kind of self-esteem, peer relationships, and a much-improved quality of life is remarkable! The concept, of bringing lonely people together so no one is lonely, is simple, yet effective, creating an environment of trust, friendship, and happiness in which social skills and confidence improve, changing lives forever.

Robert A. Weaver III, Ph.D.,
Director and Neuropsychologist

Dr. Weaver (a.k.a. Buck) is a psychologist and neuropsychologist in Wayland, MA. He developed the strength-based Weaver Center over 30 years ago, with a specialty in adolescents and young adults.

How to help children and young adults make
and keep friends.

# CREATING A
# FRIENDS GROUP

How to help children and young adults make
and keep friends.

# CREATING A
# FRIENDS GROUP

Linda Thalheimer, OTR/L MHA
and
Lau Lapides Company
Media Photography, Videography
& Voice Over Production Team

ISBN: 978-1-6653-0657-7 - Paperback
eISBN: 978-1-6653-0658-4 - eBook

These ISBNs are the property of BookLogix for the express purpose of sales and distribution of this title. BookLogix is not responsible for the writing, editing, or design/appearance of this book. The content of this book is the property of the copyright holder only. BookLogix does not hold any ownership of the content of this book and is not liable in any way for the materials contained within. The views and opinions expressed in this book are the property of the Author/ Copyright holder, and do not necessarily reflect those of BookLogix.

♾ This paper meets the requirements of ANSI/NISO Z39.48-1992 (Permanence of Paper)

Credit for photographs given to Lau Lapides Company

072023

This book is dedicated to my niece, Marissa. She was my motivation for creating The Friends Group, a group that brings together young adults who want to make and keep friends.

Thank you to the members of The Friends Group for your acceptance, kindness, and support of each other, personifying the word "friendship".

# Table of Contents

# Introduction

We could spend a day sharing stories of how hard some children try to be accepted. Many teens and young adults can initiate friendships but can't maintain them. They experience rejection or "ghosting" which can bring them to tears or lead them to seek the safety of virtual computer games, or worse. Each time rejection occurs, anxiety increases, confidence decreases and processing slows. As processing slows, the ability to learn, adapt and communicate declines. Many will convince themselves that they enjoy being alone. Others may find acceptance by peers engaging in illegal activities only to become the fall person when things go wrong. They may become vulnerable to cults and extreme political or terrorist groups who provide them with purpose and make them feel valued and appreciated. They may turn to alcohol and drugs to mask their sadness.

We are starting to see school systems take more action regarding bullying and inclusion. However, students who are not being openly mean and rejecting are not necessarily being accepting and tolerant. Parents often feel lost on how to help their unhappy, lonely child.

My understanding of social challenges took central focus nine years ago. My niece came to

Massachusetts to participate in the PAL program at Curry College and, while I knew she had some challenges, it was not until I was her family advocate that I realized she was not picking up on social cues. She did well in school and held full time jobs in the summer, but she was challenged with making friends, often feeling rejected and lonely.

One of the most important skills we addressed was how to manage anxiety so that she could stay calm enough to communicate a problem. We practiced the important social skills of maintaining eye contact, monitoring voice volume, understanding intonation, managing anxiety behaviors and learning to read social cues.

By the end of freshman year, she was making friends. By the end of her sophomore year, she was ready to transfer to a state university. Junior year was wonderful. She made friends, was being invited out by friends and was asked to be a roommate. She found a nice boyfriend. Life was wonderful.

Then came the challenge of senior year stress. As her anxiety rose, her attention to social cues and management of her anxiety behaviors declined, By the end of her senior year, most of her friends had deserted her, and her roommate had moved out. My niece was devastated.

After graduation, many of the natural opportunities to make friends had been lost. Then I had an idea. If my niece was lonely, then there had to be others who were lonely. **If I could bring lonely people together, no one would be lonely.** While the initial goal was to introduce young adults into a welcoming, safe group of friends, so much more value came from this Friends Group.

There are so few resources available to parents, family members or friends to help children or young adults find a sense of belonging, a feeling of appreciation, value and friendship, and the ability to learn new skills to make all of this easier.

It has been almost five years since I started the Friends Group. I have come to appreciate the impact of anxiety on processing, communication, and learning. I have also come to appreciate that a motivated individual can modify their anxiety behaviors in a supportive and motivational environment.

My niece is now married, has children, has friends and is happy. Her success was, in part, due to her motivation to practice social skills as identified in the "Interactive Guide to Making and Keeping Friends".

The Friends Group provides a place to feel welcome, appreciated and part of something in which one is able to gain a sense of self-awareness and confidence. Young adults, who could not carry a conversation, now can converse with relative ease. I have been amazed to observe the reduction or full elimination of repetitive anxiety behaviors. Within a setting of total acceptance, changes can often be made within weeks.

Group members look forward to seeing each other. For many, it is the first time they are receiving regular invitations to activities.

Benefits of the Friends Group
- Belonging to a group that is accepting and non-judgmental.
- Instant friendships
- Increased confidence, decreased anxiety
- Increased processing and ability to communicate
- Obtaining skills to tell stories, listen and engage in conversation.
- Participation in group activities and fun with peers

There are many different reasons people have difficulty making friends but the outcome is the same: isolation and sadness. I created this book because I wanted to share how easy it is to stimulate friendships, increase confidence, happiness and social functioning that will impact members in all aspects of their lives. Friends Groups can be started by anyone: parents, aunts, uncles, teachers, and counselors.

# Defining Your Group

The Friends Group program has been years in development, based on the primary concept of bringing people together that are motivated to make friends. My goal was to create a program that could be sustained as a volunteer, but consistent enough that it would meet the members' needs. It's time to share so that more children and young adults can benefit from the gift of friendships.

There are many options on how to structure a Friends Group. Friends Groups can be designed as dinner meetings, evening activities weekend activities or a combination of both or all three. For younger participants, they can be after-school snacks and activities and include or not include weekend activities. I have found to maintain this type of program in perpetuity, it is best to provide a consistently scheduled meeting every other week and an optional activity on every other weekend. A dinner meeting provides an easy to schedule meeting to maintain consistency while providing the leader more flexibility to meet their own scheduling and personal needs.

The day of the week for the dinner programs can be defined. or redefined after each meeting based on yours and the members' schedules. For younger groups, and those dependent on parents driving, a defined date is certainly easier.

The dinner meeting is important because most social activities involve food. A dinner meeting provides an opportunity to get to know each other without the distraction of an activity, and an opportunity to focus on important social skills: eye contact, communication skills and mealtime etiquette. Anxiety behaviors are more obvious in this sit-down setting and easier to provide feedback for change.

When starting a new group, it is helpful to introduce the group as a limited program, such as 6 weeks. This gives you greater flexibility to make changes if something is not working. It may also feel less overwhelming to start a group that is time limited. Six weeks is a long enough period for members to get to know each other and make significant social skill advancement. A fixed duration program also enhances commitment for attendance.

Optimally, the Friends Group is designed with two parts: (1) a dinner meeting and (2) a social activity. As previously identified, the dinner meeting occurs every other week. Limiting dinner meetings to 1.5 hours provides adequate time to stimulate conversations and plan for weekend activities without participants attentions waning. We scheduled our dinner meetings from 6:00-7:30 pm. Typically, we schedule these meetings on the less busy restaurant days, such as Monday or Tuesday evenings. Many of these young adults have limited food preferences, so the restaurant choices, at least for the start, are ideally ones that offer chicken fingers and hamburgers as part of the menu offering.

On the alternative week, ideally a weekend activity is scheduled. Initially, I recommend attending the weekend activities, with the goal of weaning yourself away and encouraging the young adults to manage more independently. It's important that young adults have time with other young adults and try to work things out on their own. You will get a feel when the group is ready for more independence.

For groups of younger children, an after-school program with snack time may be more appropriate. Having snack time at a table can provide similar opportunities as a dinner program for developing attention, communication, and mealtime social skills.

For younger groups, the weekend activities most often need to be supervised. You can supervise these events yourself, or have other parents take turns. Suggestions on social activities are on the next page.

The following week's dinner meeting provides a good opportunity to review the last weekend event. Discussion may include how each member felt about the activity, and process, what they liked best, and if they would want to do the activity again. If there were problems or frustrations, this is a good setting to discuss what could have been done differently to have had a better outcome.

Six weeks give you plenty of time to evaluate the mix of members, the activities, the dinner locations and pricing. You have full flexibility to make any changes without disruption for the next six week session.

Weekend events are up to you and the members to choose:

- You can choose the activities with your child.
- You can make a list and have the members choose the top three.
- You can encourage members to make suggestions and then vote for the top three.

List of ideas:

- Museums
- Aquarium
- Bowling
- Mini-golf
- Hiking
- Kayaking
- Painting/Ceramics
- Amusement parks
- Movies
- Tubing
- Video game rooms
- Board games
- Charades

Most of the time, activities will include lunch. Once the activity has been identified, specifics need to be communicated on the meeting location, start time, end time, and cost of the event. You will want to ensure there is an email/text to confirm who is attending.

# Identifying the Population

Many children have social learning challenges often identified as a spectrum disorder such as Aspergers or Autism. Other common disorders, diagnosed or not, that impact social skills include obsessive compulsive disorders, anxiety disorders, slowed processing or a lack of self-confidence. Many who find social interactions challenging  have no formal diagnosis.  Diagnosis is not important.  The only factor that is important to the membership of a Friends Group is the desire to make and keep friends. The group, by the common motivation of its members, creates an environment of acceptance and trust with peers.

Factors to consider for your group population include:

- Interests
- Age
- Gender
- Geographic Location
- Group Size

**Interests:** Because the intent of the group is to create "friends", common interests are helpful. To have a greater probability of creating common interests, marketing should focus on age and activity plans.

Generally, you can create an elementary, middle, high school, or post-high school Friends Group. However, if you have difficulty getting the age demographic you are looking for, a little flexibility, with older or younger members, is also fine. Kids that are looking for friends are much less judgmental and much more tolerant and supportive of each other regardless of age. In addition, seniors in high school can often benefit from socializing with college-age and post-college young adults as mentors. Older members are often good mentors and very supportive of younger members, sympatheitc of the challendges they are facing.

Younger Friends Group may have the added benefit for kids parents to meet new friends, as well, as they manage their kids' schedules and transportation.

My first group was started for post-college graduates. It is never too late to start a Friends Group.

**Age:** Age is much more flexible than one would think in a Friends Group. I have had successful dinner meetings with ages 13 to 35. You would think this would be unnatural and, yet, it is just the opposite. Group members were unfazed, barely acknowledging the age discrepancy and were completely appropriate with each other. Activity preferences were more dividing than age, but differences in preferences were all acknowledged with respect to each other.

**Gender**: While gender often plays a role in the preference of activities, I'd leave the group open and enable the membership to be defined by those interested in similar activities. Depending on the ages in the group, you may have to add basic rulesregarding dating others in the group. Up to now, my experience is that the group has been very respectful and focused on platonic rather than romantic or sexual relationships. But, it is always a possibility.

**Geographic Area**: You may want to choose a local demographic so that kids may be in the same school system or within a close distance to easily get together on a weekend. That being said, I have members taking trains 45 minutes each way to the meetings. One of the members moved and takes a $100 Uber ride to continue attending.

**Size:** Truly, if two members get along, you have been successful and have done a great deed. The more members, the greater the potential for scheduling activities, practicing more complex social skills and minimizing the potential for one of only two members becoming overwhelmed by the other. A group of three or four is more than enough to create a successful group. Six to ten is ideal. It's a small enough group that you can monitor interactions and large enough that weekend activities have the potential to be well attended. The more members, the greater the members feel a sense of community and acceptance. They also have greater opportunity to find that "special" friend.

# *Marketing – Finding the Members*

To market your Friends Group, you will need to define the ages, the locations, dates, and times of the meetings, types of activities, and the purpose of the group.

An example of my Friends Group advertisement on Facebook.

## Friends Group for Young Adults

A co-ed social group for young adults between the ages of 21-31 who want to make new friends. The skills involved in making friends and keeping friends are quite complex and leave many people lonely and longing for social interaction.

The Friends Group provides instant friendships and opportunities for fine tuning social skills as well as having fun with friends. We meet every other Wednesday evening from 6:00-7:30 pm at a local restaurant in the Natick-Framingham area and plan weekend events for every other week. The program is designed for high-functioning young adults either enrolled in or graduated from a college or trade school with a desire to improve their ability to make and keep friends. The next 6-week program will start Wednesday evening, March 3rd. The cost will be $99 for the three dinners. Members will pay individually at the weekend events they choose to attend.

You can also be very specific and define the weekend activities and add the cost to the program.

There are many ways to get the word out about your group.

**Word of mouth**, talking to friends, family, business associates, and social or professional organizations are excellent ways to find Friend Group members. People are eager to share information about your group and the interested party will usually reach out to you.

**Facebook** has been very successful in bringing in new members. In many ways, this is similar to word of mouth, but with a much broader range. Many people will forward your Facebook post for even greater exposure. You can also sign up for parents and school groups and put your posts on these pages as well.

**Local psychology practices** often are interested in telling their clients about your group and willing to advertise your group in their newsletters. If you know a social worker or psychologist, tell them about your group and ask if they will post your information in their office, on their website or in their newsletter.

**Guidance departments** are another resource. Send an email or visit the guidance department of your child's school, and ask if it can help you spread the word about your group. It may let you post an ad in the guidance department office or school's webpage or newsletter.

**Local e-newsletters and local newspapers** from your town will often support printing information about non-profit group opportunities.

Be specific about the age group and the types of activities so that you can attract group members who have similar interests with your individual child/young adult. For younger age groups, you may want to define a specific schedule for both dinners and activities in your advertising. You can always open membership to a greater demographic, if needed.

# Funding the Group

I designed the group with the intent that it will be affordable for the members. Many of the adult members are working minimum wage jobs and are often subsidized by parents. The cost for participation is based on one dinner and one weekend activity every other week. You can design your friends group as a prepay or pay-as-you-go or combination program. The size and age of the group will certainly influence this decision.

- **Pay-as-you- go** relies on the members to estimate, plan and bring enough money and then calculate their share at at each event. Most restaurants do not provide separate checks, so with large groups, prepay is the way to go.
- **Prepay** is the easiest and it motivates attendance at every meeting. Charging $30 to $50 a meal depending on where you are going is certainly reasonable. If there is surplus paid, you can always pay for a surprise dessert for special occasions, such as birthdays.
- **Combination** payment also works well with the meals prepaid and the weekend events pay-as-you-go.

Once you have a conistant membership, that is five or less, you may decide to change to a pay as you go. Splitting the bill at the end of the meal adds an additional social training activity. This is an opportunity to discuss tax and tips. Most of the time each will pay their own expenses. But if the group has meal costs about the same, it's an opportunity to discuss how splitting the bill evenly is an act of friendship. If one person's meal is significantly above the average it needs to be clear that the member needs to own up and add more than the rest to be fair.

If you are having the members engaged in choosing the following week activity, a combination approach to funding is a logical plan. Weekend activities will have a marked variation in cost depending on the event. Some members will want to have lunch together before or after the event, as well. It works just fine to have members pay for themselves the day of the event. However, communication is critical to define the anticipated cost of the event and the added cost for lunch. Be very specific as to how much members should bring for the day, or you may find that some members will be borrowing which is best to be avoided.

# Facilitating the Group

**First Dinner Meeting**

The number one goal is to make sure everyone feels welcome and accepted. Unless there is a very disturbing anxiety behavior, it is best to tolerate most behaviors on the first meeting to gain trust and strengthen their motivation to return.

It is not unusual when a young adult is dropped off, to hear, "My child was depressed today. It took everything to get them to participate." Or the new member may say, "I am only here because my parents told me to try, but I'm not staying for the whole event."

Fortunately, it is rare that someone does not want to come back, and I have never had anyone leave early.

**Process**: Start the meeting with the members introducing themselves with their name and something they like to do. You can continue this type of activity while waiting for a meal, having people identify their favorite color, favorite animal, favorite movie, never insisting that any one speak who does not want to, but asking them to think about an answer and to share it later. It is rare when they have been given extra time to process that they don't participate.

Some members will talk down to the table or put their hands over their mouths as they speak. This is important to address so that others can hear what they are saying.

You can say, "We really want to hear what you have to say, but we are having difficulty hearing you. Can you please look up at us when you speak or speak louder?", or "Can you please hold your hands in your lap while you speak?" If the behavior continues, let it go for now. It is more important that the person feels comfortable.

The group should expect positive reinforcement and constructive feedback of their social skills, but always in a non-threatening and non-judgmental manner. You might say to the group: "I am so happy that you have decided to be here to meet new friends. We will have lots of fun together and provide you with feedback on your social skills that may be impacting your ability to make and keep friends. We will never embarrass you. If I see a behavior that can be improved, I will try to get your eye contact and guide you to a correction, either by shaking my head or clasping my hands. I may also email you to let you know if there are some practice skills you can do at home."

Reiterating the goals of the group, helps the kids feel they are not being singled out or any different from the other members of the group when suggestions are made.

**Cell Phones:** No cell phones are allowed at the table. Explain why cell phones are being restricted:

- "You want to communicate to the others at the table that you are interested in them."
- "If you are looking at your phone, you are telling the people at the table, "I am not interested.", "I am distracted." and "I am bored."
- If you are having a discussion, and someone wants to find the answer on the cell phone, that is fine. Then the phone needs to be put away again.

I have never had anyone resist this rule, as it applies to everyone at the table. If someone forgets, a gentle reminder is all that is needed.

**Anxiety behaviors:** Everyone has anxiety behaviors. You can educate the members by saying, "When your hands are touching your face, whether it be your eyes, ears, nose, teeth or hair, it draws attention to that motion. It is distracting, and it becomes harder for others to hear what you have to say. It may also make other people uncomfortable."

You can make a general suggestion that they fold their hands or twiddle their fingers in their lap. However, they need to focus their attention on the other members, so they can't be looking down at their hands.

**Communication skills:** A topic may naturally come up or you can suggest one. Encourage listening, eye contact and asking questions to stimulate more conversation. Remind members it is important to have back and forth conversation and, after one person tells a story, to give an opportunity for someone else to speak.

**Manners:** Manners and social skills guidance around the table will often be driven by observation of less-than-appropriate behavior. It is best to present a correction as general education. For example, if you see someone reaching across the table, you can say, "Which feels more comfortable reaching across the table to get something yourself or asking someone at the table to pass it to you?" Hopefully, it will create some discussion. When the discussion is over, you will want to reiterate, "Even if it feels less comfortable to ask for help such as asking someone to pass an item on a table, it is the socially appropriate choice to make. In fact, it is better to interrupt someone who may be speaking, with a gentle "Excuse me please".

**Discussion Opportunities:**
The picking of the next dinner meeting provides opportunity for back and forth communication and compromise. Discussion can include food preferences and aversions, new restaurants and past experiences.

Choosing the weekend activity also provides opportunity for discussion. Discussion can be stimulated with a list of activity options and having members prioritize their preferences. Compromise is an important part of this program as opposed to just saying "I won't go." Members get the opportunity to express why they like some activites and not others. It should be emphasized that friends work together and compromise. The following week may be an opportunity to try the alternative suggestion.

# Providing Constructive Feedback

The Friends Group provides a unique opportunity for members to get feedback on their individual social skills. In prior relationships, if a "friend" was turned off by an anxiety behavior or "inappropriate" social skill, the member would likely be "ghosted". In this group, the members receive constructive feedback so they can modify their behaviors. If you as the leader, notice any behavior that makes you feel uncomfortable but don't want to call attention during the meeting, as it may have caused embarrassement, then providing feedback via email after the meeting is a good idea.

For most behaviors you want to change, you will find that catching the member's eyes, shaking your head, or clasping your hands together and bringing them down to your lap is all that is required to change the behavior. There is often no need to say it out loud.

At each meeting, you can reinforce the last skill and add a new one, based on the skill set of your group. Skills may include enhancing eye contact, voice volume, intonation, taking smaller bites, or eating with one's mouth closed. Let's go through some of the social skills that are likely to come up so that you can help members recognize them and change.

**Eye Contact:** Eye contact tells the listener, "I am interested. I am focused on what you are saying. I am not distracted. I am sincere". Unfortunately, lack of eye contact says just the opposite even if that is not intended. It says, "I am not listening. I am not focused on what you are saying. I am distracted. I am bored. I am anxious." When the group understands the importance of eye contact, feedback to enhance this skill becomes welcomed.

**Volume of voice:** In the beginning, members tend to be quiet and not speak loud enough for others to hear them. When members get comfortable, they may get too loud. Discussing the importance of voice volume relative to the event is important. If members are too quiet, talking down to the table or covering their mouths, a discussion on how sound travels can be a diplomatic way to address this issue. For example, "If you are trying to talk to someone behind you, how loud do you have to talk for them to hear vs. if you turned around and spoke face to face." You can try this, if needed. You can ask the members how they feel when they can't hear or understand what another person is saying. You can also talk about the volume of noise in the room and the need to talk louder and more directly in louder environments and softer in quieter settings.

**Intonation:** The rise and fall of our voices make what we say more interesting and often provide greater meaning of the sentence than the words themselves. You may want to discuss the importance of intonation if one or more of your members are talking in monotone. It is difficult to identify mood or interest without intonation. Even a word as simple as "hi" can express excitement or boredom. You can have members take turns talking in monotone and then saying something with inflection to emphasize this point.

You may also want to discuss the importance of intonation when a member does not pick up on someone's joke or sarcasm. Or worse, when a member feels insulted by another intending a joke.

You may want to explain that it is rare for people to be directly mean to one another. When it seems like someone is saying the opposite of what you would expect, this is called sarcasm or a joke and is intended to be funny.

Set the stage with the concept of being at an event they hate and asked, "Are you having a good time" and the response is "Ya, great.". It is obvious that "Ya, great," is the opposite of the intented meaning. Have members try to come up with with scenerios when sarcasm may be common and how it would sound.

The goal is to help members become aware of intonation, its impact on communication and how easy it is to modify.

Taking large bites:
Taking large bites creates two problems. The first is the embarrassing appearance of trying to get food into the mouth neatly and the second is then it requires chewing with the mouth open to get the food down to size. If you see someone taking too large bites, you can say...."It's important to take small bites onto your fork. Sometimes, it will require you

to cut your food smaller." If it continues, discuss the concept of videotaping oneself at home so that they can become more aware of their habit and how it may make others uncomfortable. Always be aware to do this in a non-judgmental, supportive manner.

**Chewing with one's mouth open:**

If someone is chewing with their mouth open, you can say, "Most people can't tell if they are eating with their mouth open or closed. There are several social issues with eating with your mouth open. The first is that people see your food which is not attractive. Second, chewing becomes more audible which is distracting and even anxiety producing for others. Third, if you begin to talk, food tends to spit out." After the meal or via email, you can again suggest, the concept of videotaping themselves chewing during meals to help them become more aware and better able to break this habit.

# Conversation Starters

You will likely find that you will be the facilitator of conversation at the meetings. Once the dinner meetings become routine, open ended questions about work, last weekend activity or specific interests work well.

As the group members gets more comfortable with each other, you can provide opportunity for members to discuss challenges at work or home for their "friends" to provide support and guidance. This is an opportunity for you to help them identify when their problems are less to do with what they did, but rather how others interpret their behaviors. Sometimes a recommendation for third party involvement may help them enjoy a better work environment.

Some learning styles are very literal and the subtleties of political correctness can be lost. You may find inappropriate questions harmlessly asked. It is very rare for these young adults to be intentionally mean. It is important not to overreact, but to help them become more aware of how what they say can be interpreted by others.

Other important topics for conversation include social media, dating apps, texting. It is critical that your group understand that anything they say in writing can and often will be held against them. They must also know that even when they believe they are in love, never to send naked pictures of themselves as these pictures become the property of the other person.

# Social Guidelines for Communication

It is important to constantly reinforce good "friendship" behavior.

The group will be sending out notices via email and/or text about dinner meetings and weekend activities. It is important that members respond to all communications and do so within 24 hours. Members need to know communication is important. They don't need to answer "yes"; a "no" is perfectly acceptable. But an answer needs to be sent.  No answer is not only disrespectful but will cause the rest of the group to worry that something is wrong. After all, group members are friends and do care about one another. A text can take two seconds to acknowledge; there is no reason to ignore a member's text.

If a member asks another member to a private activity, that is fine and encouraged. The other member can always say "no". General rule is you can ask twice, either for a different day or a different event. If the answer is still no, stop texting, and we can always try to get feedback from the other member for learning purposes as to why the answerwas "no".

If a member has committed to a dinner or weekend event and suddenly can't attend, it is imperative that they communicate with the leader or one of the other members so that the group does not worry or wait needlessly for someone who is not arriving. Making sure that everyone has each other's cell phone numbers is important so that this type of communication can take place.

While communication rules seem basic and common sense, social etiquette and courtesies do need to be stated and reinforced. Often members feel uncomfortable responding or don't know how to answer if they are uncertain of the answer. When you find that members are not responding to eachother in a timely manner, or at all, bring it up as a question to the group. "Why do you think some people might not respond to a text or email or not communicate if they are going to be late or not attend?" Then discuss how lack of communication impacts other members. This is an important learning opportunity.

# Unique Situational Opportunities

When bad things happen, an opportunity presents...

At one of our dinner meetings, one of our members was late, which was very much out of the ordinary for him. It turns out he went to the wrong location. When I called, and he realized he was in the wrong restaurant, I could hear the panic in his voice. He had been dropped off via an Uber, with no easy form of transportation to correct. I had everyone hop in my car and, with the cell phone on speakerphone, we talked with him while we drove to pick him up. He made a comment that the directions in the email were not clear. I took this as an opportunity to discuss asking for clarification or help. I asked everyone in the car, "If someone in the group called or texted you to ask for clarification of location, would you feel bothered or imposed upon?" The answers were universally no. I asked if it might even have made you feel good, useful, or helpful? The answers were universally yes. We all have experienced the hesitation to ask someone else for clarification and ended up late or in the wrong location because we did not ask. This was a critical learning opportunity for all, not only asking for directions, but also asking for help.

At another meeting, a member came in upset; she was afraid she was going to lose her job. After listening to her description, it became clear to me that the problem was not as much what she was doing, but rather the misinterpretation of her behavior by the staff. It is not uncommon for those who have difficulty making and keeping friends to also have some challenges at work. When a rule changes, it creates anxiety, as the new rule now needs to be fully understood as it replaced the old one. When the employee starts asking detailed questions, they are often identified as a troublemaker or for being disrespectful. For example, if the manager states, " The dress code is changing from black pants to blue." The employee may need to ask, "Does this mean light blue, dark blue, Tye-dyed blue? Does this include leggings, sweatpants, nice pants or jeans? " You can see how this might make an administrator feel like the employee is mocking or defiant and yet, the employee is just trying to make sure the rule is fully understood to mitigage anxiety.

It was not a surprise to find other members in the group confiding in situations in which they were not understood at their place of work, as well. While you won't be able to solve all the problems, helping the members understand the problem reduces their burden. You may recommend that they seek a liason to communicate to employers on their behalf to help create a better work environment for all.

# Leadership Opportunities

As members get comfortable with the group and the routine, you will start to recognize unique strengths and interests of the individual members. Whenever possible, when setting up the weekend events, identify someone in the group to take a leadership role. For example, if the activity requires using public transportation, ask the member who uses public transportation most frequently to help. Have this member identify the stations and make themselves available to the other members who may be anxious or unfamiliar with public transportation.

If the activity is hiking, ask the hiker in the group to make a list and distribute it to the group as to what they should wear and what to bring in their backpacks.

Leaders will start to emerge. This is a great opportunity to expand your friends group to develop a mentor program. The goal of the mentor program is to teach organization, communication and leadership skills. Offering to pay the leader for the activity that they are supervising, is highly motivating.

**Skills and responsibilities of the mentor:**

- Sending out emails defining weekend events including meeting location, start and end time, and cost of the event. If special clothing or accessories are needed, the mentor would need to include this information in the email.
- Confirming RSVP's, reconfirming attendance prior to the event and making sure all who RSVP'd are present at the event.
- Identifying a meet up place and time should they get separated and reconfirming that all members have the other's cell phone numbers in their phones.

You will want to be on all the email and text messaging so that you can monitor and educate, supplementing as necessary.

If you have an additional funding source, having two mentors is even better, so if one isn't able to show up, you have a backup. Creating a mentor program will eventually free up more of your time and enable the group to participate in more activities.

## Summary

Friends Groups provide an opportunity for kids to have instant friends in an environment of acceptance and tolerance. This enables changes in behavior that enhance abilities to process information, communicate and make and keep friends.

If you can find just one other person who has similar interests to your child, you have been successful. The group basically insures that its participants are motivated to make friends.

Some have questioned me about liability. I have driven members to meetings and to events, and I have hosted meetings in my home. If I am at fault for an accident, yes, it will be my liability. That being said, this is not a risk you need to take. Parents or members are responsible for their own transportation, and I do have members taking Ubers to and from our meetings. Members will often drive each other as you would expect friends to do. I do not restrict alcohol from our dinner meetings, but I do not drink at the meetings, and I do not encourage it. I would limit members to one drink, but have not had to. Interestingly, while some of-age members do order an alcoholic drink with their meal, they have self-limited.

Creating a group is a gift to the members. You are about to change more than one life in a way that will warm your heart. You will be awed by the impact of friendship. Thank you if you are taking on this role.

If you have questions or you want to share a challenge or success, please leave a message on our website, www.makingandkeepingfriends.com.
I would love to hear from you.

*Linda Thalheimer*

**OTR/L, MHA**

www.ingramcontent.com/pod-product-compliance
Lightning Source LLC
Chambersburg PA
CBHW051249020426
42333CB00025B/3130